P9-DBT-135

WATER CREATURES

TERRIFYING & UGLY SEA CREATURES

Per Christiansen

Gareth Stevens
Publishing

Please visit our web site at www.garethstevens.com.
For a free color catalog describing Gareth Stevens Publishing's
list of high-quality books, call 1-800-542-2595 (USA)
or 1-800-387-3178 (Canada).
Gareth Stevens Publishing's fax: 1-877-542-2596

Library of Congress Cataloging-in-Publication Data
available upon request from publisher.

ISBN-10: 0-8368-9221-6 (lib. bdg.)
ISBN-13: 978-0-8368-9221-5 (lib. bdg.)

This North American edition first published in 2009 by
Gareth Stevens Publishing
A Weekly Reader® Company
1 Reader's Digest Road
Pleasantville, NY 10570-7000 USA

Copyright © 2009 by Amber Books, Ltd.
Produced by Amber Books Ltd., Bradley's Close
74–77 White Lion Street
London N1 9PF, U.K.

All illustrations © International Masters Publishers AB except 7 ©
Amber Books Ltd.

Project Editor: James Bennett
Design: Tony Cohen

Gareth Stevens Senior Managing Editor: Lisa M. Herrington
Gareth Stevens Editor: Joann Jovinelly
Gareth Stevens Creative Director: Lisa Donovan
Gareth Stevens Designer: Paul Bodley

Printed in the United States of America

1 2 3 4 5 6 7 8 9 10 09 08

7/10

Contents

Continents of the World

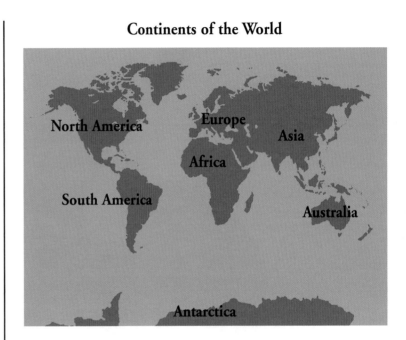

The world is divided into seven continents — North America, South America, Europe, Africa, Asia, Australia, and Antarctica. In this book, the area where each animal lives is shown in blue, while all land is shown in green.

Words that appear in the glossary are printed in **boldface** type the first time they occur in the text.

Anglerfish

On top of its head, the anglerfish has three long threadlike spines. It wiggles these spines to **lure** its **prey** closer.

Some anglerfish swim through shallow seas, but this one lives near the seabed. It has thick, fleshy fins for moving around on the ocean floor.

Like many deep-sea fish, the anglerfish has a huge mouth. It can swallow any passing prey.

The anglerfish has a small body. Even so, its stomach can stretch to hold a prey animal nearly half the size of the fish itself!

Most anglerfish are small, but the one seen here is a giant. It can grow to more than 6 feet (1.8 meters) and can weigh up to 100 pounds (45 kilograms).

The female anglerfish lays its eggs in a clear, jelly-like sheet. This huge sheet can be as much as 3 feet (91 centimeters) wide and 30 feet (9.1 m) long! Since **predators** dislike the taste of the sheet, the eggs are safe from harm.

1 The anglerfish has speckled skin, which helps **camouflage** it against the ocean floor. It lies without moving for hours, waiting for its prey.

2 From a distance, the anglerfish's spines look like worms. Fish think they are worms and are lured closer. When the fish gets close, the anglerfish opens its huge mouth and swallows its prey in one mighty gulp!

Anglerfish live in coastal waters around Europe, the east coast of the Americas, and the Mediterranean Sea.

Conger Eel

The conger eel has large **pectoral**, or front, fins for steering. Like other eels, it lacks **dorsal**, or rear, fins.

The conger eel has large **gills**, which absorb oxygen from the water. Unlike many eels, it does not swim into rivers and streams.

The conger eel does not have scales. Its skin is tough and leathery.

The conger eel has a large mouth and a strong jaw lined with sharp teeth. It feeds on squid, crayfish, and smaller fish.

The name conger eel is used for many different large eels. The largest ones live in the Atlantic Ocean and Mediterranean Sea. They can grow up to 10 feet (3 m) and can weigh as much as 250 pounds (113 kg)!

Size

1 Conger eels are a popular food in many countries. This fisherman has just caught a large eel in the northern Atlantic Ocean.

2 The fisherman removes the eel's head to prepare it for sale.

3 Suddenly, the eel gives a jolt. Although the eel is headless, its nerves still work. It clamps its jaws around the fisherman's hand. He cries out in pain. This eel was supposed to be dead!

Where in the World

Conger eels live on the sandy and rocky bottoms of European coasts. The adults move farther out to sea for breeding.

Gray Reef Shark

The gray reef shark's body is shaped like a **torpedo**. Its **streamlined** form helps it swim rapidly after its prey.

Rows of triangular, razor-sharp teeth line the shark's mouth. When a tooth becomes worn, it falls out and is replaced by a new one.

The gray reef shark has a white belly and a dark gray back. This coloring makes the shark difficult to see.

Two large pectoral fins steer the shark swiftly through the water.

Large gray reef sharks can grow to about 7 feet (2 m) and can weigh several hundred pounds. Giant gray reef sharks may measure almost 9 feet (2.7 m)!

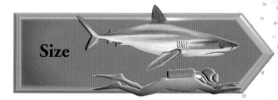

Size

1 The gray reef shark is an intelligent and curious predator. It watches a scuba diver as he swims closer.

2 The shark prepares to defend its territory. It swiftly arches its back, lifts its head, and swings its tail.

3 Suddenly, the shark attacks. Its many teeth rip open the diver's arm. Luckily, gray reef sharks rarely attack humans.

The gray reef shark lives in many parts of the Pacific and Indian Oceans. They are often found on **coral reefs** or near **atolls**.

Hatchetfish

Hatchetfish have bulging, egg-shaped eyes. Their eyes are very large, but they look in only one direction—straight up!

The hatchetfish's tail is much thinner than its body. They do not have thick, muscular tails like many other fish, such as herring. Hatchetfish swim slowly.

The fish's mouth is huge and lined with long, sharp teeth. The hatchetfish can swallow prey almost the same size as itself.

The hatchetfish got its name because its deep, flat body looks like the blade of a hatchet.

Like many deep-sea creatures, hatchetfish are small. Most are 3 to 8 inches (8 to 20 cm) long. Giant hatchetfish can grow up to 2 feet (61 cm)!

Size

Did You Know?

The deep sea is almost totally dark, so many deep-sea creatures produce light. In hatchetfish, light is produced by organs called photophores. These fish use light to attract prey, possibly **mates**, and to scare off predators.

1 Like many deep-sea creatures, hatchetfish can send light from their body! They use the light not only to scare off predators, but also to lure prey.

2 The strange blue-green light attracts this shrimp. It swims closer to investigate. Seconds later, the shrimp discovers that the light comes from a hungry hatchetfish!

3 The shrimp is large, but the hatchetfish has a huge mouth. It swallows the shrimp whole!

Where in the World

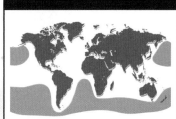

There are many kinds of hatchetfish in the world's oceans. Because they prefer warm water, most are found in the **tropics**.

Lamprey

Lampreys have leathery skin that is covered by slime. They have seven gills on each side of their bodies.

Instead of a mouth, the lamprey has a wide sucker lined with rows of sharp teeth. The lamprey uses its teeth to saw into the flesh of other fish!

Brown patches cover much of the lamprey's skin, camouflaging the fish.

The lamprey's body is long, like an eel's body. Lampreys are not related to eels. They belong to a group called the jawless fishes.

Lampreys vary in size. Adults can be from 5 to 40 inches (13 to 102 cm) long. Although they swim well, most lampreys travel as passengers, attached to the fish on which they feed.

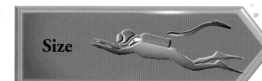

Jawless fish first appeared in the world's oceans more than 500 million years ago! Instead of a jaw, fish belonging to this **ancient** group have sucker-like mouths. They use their suckers to gnaw off pieces of flesh from their prey.

1 ▷ The lamprey is a **parasite**. It swims up to a fish and attaches its sucker to the fish's body.

2 ▷ Then the lamprey gnaws through the fish's skin. The lamprey sucks out the fish's body fluids!

3 ▷ When the lamprey has eaten its fill, it swims away. The wounded fish sinks, bleeding in the water.

The lamprey is common in the northern Atlantic Ocean. Another jawless fish that lives in these waters is the hagfish.

Oarfish

The dorsal, or back, fin of the oarfish runs the entire length of its body. The beginning of the dorsal fin is extremely tall.

The oarfish has a small head with large eyes. It does not have any visible teeth.

The oarfish's silvery-blue body is very long and thin. It also has many dark stripes, which act to camouflage the fish.

The fish's pectoral, or front, fins are long and thin and look like oars.

The oarfish is a true giant among **bony fish**. It regularly reaches lengths of 20 feet (6 m). A record-breaking oarfish measured a whopping 35 feet (11 m)!

The oarfish belongs to a group of fish called *Regalecidae*. That name comes from the Latin word for "royal." Scientists now believe that old stories once told about sea serpents are most likely based on rare sightings of oarfish.

1 The oarfish is rarely seen alive. It lives deep in the ocean to depths of about 3,500 feet (1,070 m). It feeds on small fish, crayfish, and squid. The oarfish chases its prey at high speeds. It uses its long dorsal fin for swimming, which is unusual among fish.

2 Occasionally, fishermen get an oarfish caught in their **trawl nets**. In Bermuda, fishermen have reported oarfish coming to the surface at night. They often do this if they are sick or injured.

Although the oarfish is found in most oceans, scientists know little about its **habitat**.

Portuguese Man-of-War

The Portuguese man-of-war looks like one animal, but it is a colony of small **polyps**.

The large air bladder is the only part of the Portuguese man-of-war that is visible above the water. The rest of the body is under the surface.

Beneath the colony are hundreds of long, thread-like **tentacles**. These feelers can deliver nasty, painful stings!

The Portuguese man-of-war is usually a beautiful blue or blue-green color. Its name comes from a type of sailing ship of the 1300s and 1400s.

The tentacles of a Portuguese man-of-war can grow to enormous lengths. Normally, tentacles are between 3 to 4 feet (0.9 to 1.2 m) long, but Portuguese man-of-war have been found with nearly 30-foot (9.1-m) tentacles!

Size

Did You Know?

Some of the Portuguese man-of-war polyps form the air bladder, which keeps the colony afloat. Other polyps form the body, and still others form the stinging tentacles. The tentacles trap prey, which is then divided among the entire colony.

1 A Portuguese man-of-war is only partly visible as it floats on the surface of the ocean. People often do not notice the animal until they are caught in its tentacles.

2 An unlucky swimmer who gets caught in the mesh of stinging tentacles is in serious trouble. The stings are terribly painful. A swimmer could lose **consciousness** and drown.

Portuguese man-of-war live in **temperate** and **tropical** oceans around the world.

Stonefish

The huge, ugly head of the stonefish is the only part of its body that is visible as it hides on the seafloor.

Along its back stand thirteen sharp spines, each equipped with a **venom gland**. These spines inject a powerful poison into the stonefish's prey.

The stonefish's skin is tough and looks like stone. It is brown or green and is often covered with orange patches. The stonefish blends easily into its surroundings.

The stonefish's fins are wide and heavy. It uses them to dig into the rocky seabed to bury itself.

The stonefish is among the deadliest fish in the world. The spines on its back can inject venom that causes extreme pain and often leads to death. It can reach about 15 inches (38 cm) in length.

Size

A stonefish hides among stones and coral on a reef. Half-buried in sand, it is very hard to see. The stonefish senses the movement of this swimmer and raises its deadly spines.

> 1

Where in the World

The stonefish lives in shallow tropical waters in the Indian and Pacific Oceans. It is common along the northern coasts of Australia.

> 2

The base of each spine is full of venom. As the swimmer's finger touches the spine, the seal at the top is broken. The venom (shown in blue) is injected into the finger, causing severe pain.

Sturgeon

The sturgeon's nose is flat and shaped like a triangle. It uses its nose to search for food by stirring up soft mud on the ocean floor.

Most fish are covered in scales, but the sturgeon is covered in tough, bony plates called **scutes**.

Bluish or greenish-black spots cover the sturgeon's back. Its underside is white.

Four long, sensitive threads called **barbels** hang from the sturgeon's nose. The fish uses these barbels to locate prey.

The Atlantic sturgeon shown here can grow to 15 feet (4.6 m) long and may weigh more than 2,000 pounds (907 kg). The Beluga sturgeon is even bigger and may reach 17 feet (5.2 m) and weigh more than 3,000 pounds (1,361 kg)!

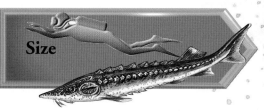

Size

1 Sturgeons are fierce predators. They are born in **brackish** water, where they live for up to six years. They feed on small animals, such as crayfish and clams. Sturgeons hunt for prey near the seabed. This sturgeon chases after a smaller fish.

2 The sturgeon's barbels are very sensitive and act as its "eyes." When prey such as this fish touches the barbels, the sturgeon opens its mouth to swallow the fish whole.

Where in the World

The Atlantic sturgeon lives along the Atlantic coast of North America. Other sturgeons live in waters throughout the Northern Hemisphere.

Toadfish

A toadfish's skin often lacks scales. Its skin color varies. It is usually spotted to blend in with its surroundings. Prey cannot see it hiding.

Some toadfish have poisonous spines along their gills and back. Despite their scary appearance, most toadfish are not dangerous to humans.

The toadfish's fins are large. It sometimes uses them to crawl on the ocean floor.

Toadfish are relatively small, usually about 12 inches (30 cm) long. Some are much smaller, reaching only 5 to 6 inches (13 to 15 cm) in length.

1 This Caribbean fisherman reaches into a lobster pot. He does not know that a toadfish is inside.

2 The fisherman shouts in pain. As he pulls his hand from the pot, he sees the toadfish's spikes stuck into his hand.

Did You Know?

Toadfish can actually sing! The males vibrate their swim bladders to produce purring "songs," which attract females. Toadfish sometimes purr when touched, probably to scare predators. The toadfish can then make a hasty escape.

Where in the World

Toadfish live in much of the world but are most common in the waters around Central and South America.

Wolffish

The wolffish has large eyes that stick out. The fish can see well when hunting prey.

The wolffish's dorsal, or back, fin is long. Its pale blue color and dark stripes provide camouflage. Predators cannot see the fish easily.

Rows of strong, pointed teeth line the wolffish's jaw. They can give a nasty bite.

The wolffish has large pectoral, or front, fins. It uses them to steer through the water.

The wolffish is a large predator. Normally, it grows to a length of about 3 feet (91 cm). Giants measuring 5 feet (1.5 m) and weighing a whopping 55 pounds (25 kg) have been caught.

Size

1. The wolffish is active at night, prowling the ocean floor for prey. During the day, it hides among rocks on the ocean floor.

2. The wolffish sometimes feeds on small fish, but its main diet is crayfish and clams. Here it has spotted a crab. The crab cannot defend itself.

3. With its powerful teeth, the wolffish crushes the crab. The wolffish can fend off most large or small predators.

Where in the World

Wolffish live in the northern Atlantic Ocean and around the coasts of the United Kingdom.

Crown-of-Thorns Starfish

Anywhere from twelve to nineteen arms extend from the starfish's body.

The crown-of-thorns starfish is covered in sharp spines. Its skin is pale blue, creating a contrast to its red spines. The color red is a warning to keep away!

Special suckers line the underside of arm. The starfish uses these suckers to move around.

The crown-of-thorns starfish starts out no larger than a grain of sand but grows to be the size of a dinner plate! Large individuals measure more than 15 inches (38 cm) from tip to tip.

Size

1 The crown-of-thorns starfish is common on coral reefs, where it feeds on the corals. New divers often attempt to pick it up.

2 New divers are in for a nasty surprise! The spines are needle-sharp and easily poke through skin. The crown-of-thorns starfish is **venomous**. Its venom causes an intense burning pain that can last for hours. The venom may even cause nausea and vomiting!

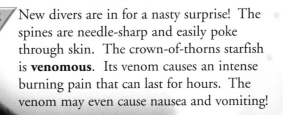

Where in the World

The crown-of-thorns starfish lives in warm oceans around the world. It is most common off the coasts of Australia.

Bobbit Worm

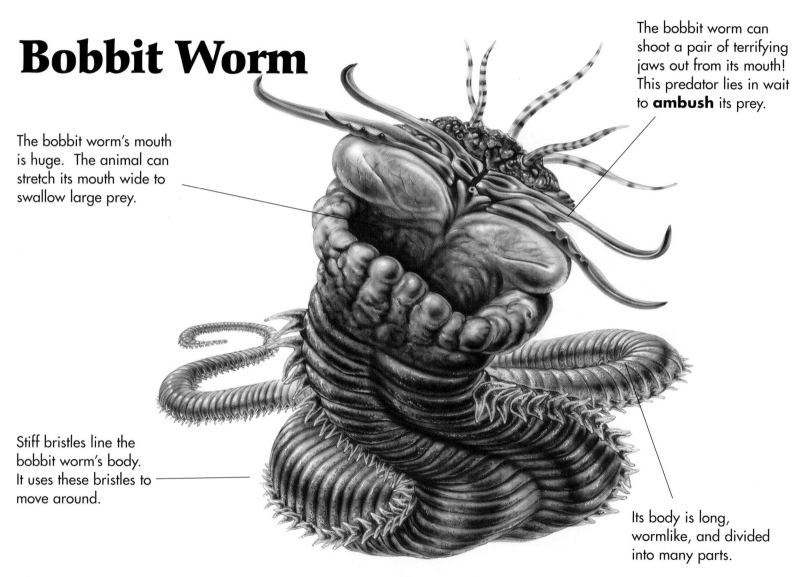

The bobbit worm's mouth is huge. The animal can stretch its mouth wide to swallow large prey.

The bobbit worm can shoot a pair of terrifying jaws out from its mouth! This predator lies in wait to **ambush** its prey.

Stiff bristles line the bobbit worm's body. It uses these bristles to move around.

Its body is long, wormlike, and divided into many parts.

Bobbit worms can grow to a length of 15 inches (38 cm). They live in **burrows**. The only part of the worm that is visible is the head.

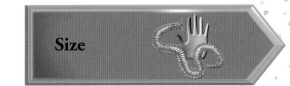
The bobbit worm is a fierce predator to small animals. It lies in wait in its burrow. If a suitable animal passes by, the worm shoots out of its burrow and grabs it with its huge jaws. Sometimes the attack is so violent that the prey is bitten in half!

1 Bobbit worms are common in shallow waters with sandy bottoms. They also live on coral reefs, which are popular places for divers. This diver has just grabbed a lobster.

2 A bobbit worm lies in wait close to the lobster. Instead of striking the lobster, the bobbit worm bites the diver's hand. The shocked diver now has a very sore finger!

Where in the World

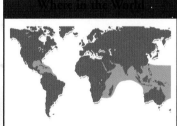

The bobbit worm lives in the tropical waters of the Indian and Pacific Oceans.

Glossary

ambush — to make a surprise attack from a hiding place

ancient — from a very early time in history

atolls — coral islands made up of a reef surrounding a shallow pond

barbels — long, sensitive threads that hang from the head of a sturgeon and act as its "eyes."

bony fish — a group of fishes with a skeleton made mostly of bones, not cartilage

brackish — having a mix of fresh and salt water

burrows — holes made in the ground by animals for shelter and protection

camouflage — surface coloring that helps an animal blend in with the plants, rocks, and soil where it lives

cartilage — a firm, flexible body tissue

consciousness — the state of being awake and aware

coral reefs — coral ridges, lying above or near the surface of the sea, made from the skeletons of sea animals

dorsal — refers to the upper back, or dorsum, of a fish

endangered — at risk of dying out

gills — parts of a fish or shark used for taking in oxygen under water

habitat — the natural environment of a living thing

larvae — young, developing animals such as fish and insects

lure — to draw closer, to attract strongly

mates — a pair of animals that join together to produce offspring

parasite — a plant or an animal that lives in or on another living thing

pectoral — behind the head of a fish or shark

polyps — animals without backbones that have tube-like hollow bodies with central mouths surrounded by tentacles

predators — animals that hunt other animals for food

prey — an animal hunted and killed for food

primitive — belonging to an early form of an animal species

scutes — a thickened horny or bony plate on an animal's back

streamlined — having a smooth shape designed to move easily through water or air

temperate — marked by temperatures that are neither very hot nor very cold

tentacles — long, sensitive feelers used to touch and grasp

torpedo — a cigar-shaped missile fired by ships and submarines through the sea

trawl nets — large nets shaped like cones that are dragged along the ocean floor to catch fish

tropical — referring to the hottest regions of the world, with lush plant life and a lot of rain

tropics — an area of Earth that is near the equator where it is always warm

venom gland — the part of the fish where venom, or poison, is produced

venomous — containing poison

For More Information

Books

The Incredible Hunt for the Giant Squid. Incredible Deep-Sea Adventures (series). Bradford Matsen (Enslow, 2003)

Octopuses and Squid. Scary Creatures (series). Gerald Legg (Franklin Watts, 2004)

Sea Monsters. A Canadian Museum of Nature Book (series). Stephen Cumbaa (Kids Can Press, 2007)

Sea Monsters. Up Close (series). Paul Harrison (Rosen/PowerKids Press, 2008)

Sharks. Scary Creatures (series). Penny Clarke (Franklin Watts, 2002)

Fierce Water Creatures. Nature's Monsters (series). Gerrie McCall (Gareth Stevens, 2005)

Web Sites

BBC – Science & Nature – Sea Monsters
www.bbc.co.uk/sn/prehistoric_life/tv_radio/wwseamonsters

Creatures From the Deep
www.thedeepbook.org

National Museum of Natural History – Marine Ecosystems
www.mnh.si.edu/museum/VirtualTour/Tour/First/Marine /index.html

Science News for Kids — Lampreys
www.sciencenewsforkids.org/articles/20051116/Note2.asp

Six of the Sea's Scariest Monsters
www.quazen.com/Science/Zoology/Six-of-the-Seas-Scariest-Monsters.79077

World of Sharks
www.pbs.org/wgbh/nova/sharks/world

Publisher's note to educators and parents: Our editors have carefully reviewed these web sites to ensure that they are suitable for children. Many web sites change frequently, however, and we cannot guarantee that a site's future contents will continue to meet our high standards of quality and educational value. Be advised that children should be closely supervised whenever they access the Internet.

Index